My Science Library

I Use a Mouse

by Kelli Hicks

Science Content Editor:
Kristi Lew

www.rourkeclassroom.com

Science content editor: Kristi Lew

A former high school teacher with a background in biochemistry and more than 10 years of experience in cytogenetic laboratories, Kristi Lew specializes in taking complex scientific information and making it fun and interesting for scientists and non-scientists alike. She is the author of more than 20 science books for children and teachers.

www.rourkeclassroom.com

Photo credits: Cover © luchschen, Catalin Petolea, Diamond_Images, ussr; Page 5 © Rob Marmion; Page 6 © urfin; Page 7 © ARTEKI; Page 8 © Rennaulka; Page 9 © ArchMan; Page 10 © Dragana Francuski Tolimir; Page 11 © sergei telegin; Page 13 © STILLFX; Page 15 © Catalin Petolea; Page 17 © ZTS; Page 18 © urfin; Page 19 © ArchMan; Page 20 © Yobidaba, Rennaulka; Page 21 © ZTS

Editor: Jeanne Sturm

Cover and page design by Nicola Stratford, bdpublishing.com

Library of Congress Cataloging-in-Publication Data

Hicks, Kelli L.
I use a mouse / Kelli Hicks.
 p. cm. -- (My science library)
Includes bibliographical references and index.
ISBN 978-1-61741-742-9 (Hard cover) (alk. paper)
ISBN 978-1-61741-944-7 (Soft cover)
1. Computers--Juvenile literature. 2. Mice (Computers)--Juvenile literature. 3. Keyboards (Electronics)--Juvenile literature. I. Title.
TK7885.5.H53 2012
004--dc22
                    2011003871

Rourke Publishing
Printed in China,
  Power Printing Company Ltd
  Guangdong Province
042011
042011LP

www.rourkeclassroom.com - rourke@rourkepublishing.com
Post Office Box 643328 Vero Beach, Florida 32964

Table of Contents

Getting Started

I press the power button and turn on my computer. I use a tool with two buttons that I move with my hand. Do you know what it is?

I Use a Mouse

I use a mouse! I use it to tell the computer what to do. I click a button on the mouse with my finger to send a **message** into the computer.

I look at the **monitor** and I see an arrow. The arrow helps me to know where I'm clicking. I use the mouse to move the arrow.

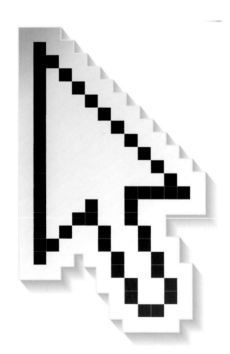

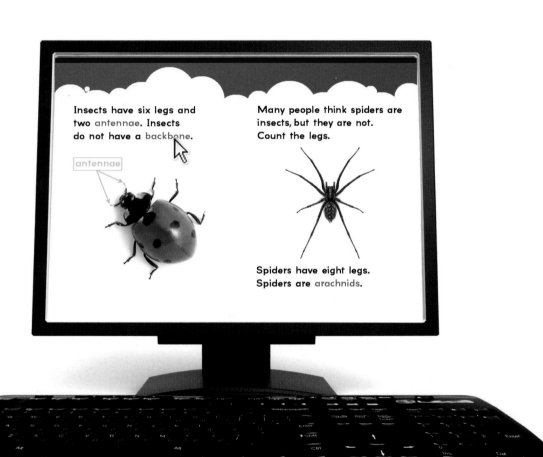

Insects have six legs and two antennae. Insects do not have a backbone.

antennae

Many people think spiders are insects, but they are not. Count the legs.

Spiders have eight legs. Spiders are arachnids.

I Use a Keyboard

Sometimes I use a **keyboard** to give the computer **instructions**. The keyboard has numbers, letters, and symbols on it.

I use the arrow keys on the keyboard when I am playing a game.

I Can Do More

I use the mouse to find science facts on the computer. I use the keyboard to write about what I have learned.

The Water Cycle

When the Sun warms rivers, oceans, and lakes, water vapor forms. The water vapor rises, then cools, becoming water droplets.

I use a **printer** when I want to have a copy of the information. The printer uses ink to put the words on the paper.

When the Sun warms
rivers, oceans, and lakes
, water vapor forms.
The water cools, becoming
, then cools, becoming
water droplets.

I like to read stories about science on the computer, and I use the mouse to help me keep my place. I use it to move to the next page of the story.

From flowers to leaves,
the trees turn green.

I use the speakers to hear sounds from the computer. I use a mouse to make the sound louder or softer. What can you do with a mouse?

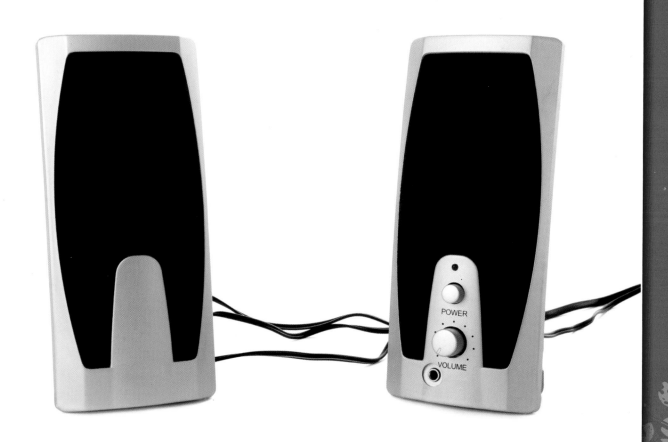

SHOW What You Know

1. What is a mouse?

2. How can the keyboard be useful?

3. What are some things the mouse can help you do?

Glossary

instructions (in-STRUHK-shuhnz): lessons or directions on how to do something

keyboard (KEE-bord): the set of keys or buttons on a computer

message (MESS-ij): information sent to someone or something

monitor (MON-uh-tur): the visual display of a computer

printer (PRINT-ur): a machine that uses ink to produce words or pictures on a page

Index

Websites

www.computerlabkids.com

www.edutainingkids.com/articles/masteringmouse.html

www.kidsdomain.com/brain/computer/lesson/comp_les1.html

www.kids-online.net/learn/c_n_l.html

library.thinkquest.org/5862/

www.pysycache.org/

About the Author

Kelli Hicks can use a mouse and is always trying to learn more about the other parts of her computer. She lives in Tampa, Florida, with her husband, her two children Mackenzie and Barrett, and their golden retriever Gingerbread.

24